Clever
Crafts
for
Little
Fingers

fun with
PAPER

Annalees Lim

WAYLAND

First published in 2012 by Wayland

Copyright © Wayland 2012

Wayland
Hachette Children's Books
338 Euston Road
London NW1 3BR

Wayland Australia
Level 17/207 Kent Street
Sydney NSW 2000

Editor: Victoria Brooker
Designer: Lisa Peacock
Step-by-step photographs: Simon Pask, N1 Studios
Images used for creative graphics: Shutterstock
Cover picture: Thanks to Malachy Burke

British Library Cataloguing in Publication Data

Lim, Annalees.
  Fun with paper. -- (Clever crafts for little fingers)
  1. Paper work--Juvenile literature.
  I. Title II. Series
  745.5'4-dc23

ISBN: 978 0 7502 6829 5

Printed in China

Wayland is a division of Hachette Children's Books,
an Hachette UK Company.
www.hachette.co.uk

For templates and more craft tips
and activities, go to:
www.wayland.co.uk/downloads

Contents

Fun with Paper

You can find paper everywhere in different sizes, shapes, colours and textures. From coloured paper to newspaper, tissue paper to wrapping paper, paper can be found all around your home.

Transforming your piece of paper is easy. In this book, you will learn how to decorate paper using paints and colouring pens; join paper with glue, sticky tape and staples; and shape your paper by folding, tearing and cutting.

Paper is the perfect material to be creative with. Once you learn the basics, there is no end to the paper crafts you can make. Try adapting the projects in this book using different designs, colours or by adding glitter and sparkles.

Wrapping paper

Newspaper

Torn paper

In this book, you will need:

Colouring pens
Any shape or thickness. You don't have to follow the colours used in this book.

Paint
To decorate your crafts. Use poster paints or acrylic paints.

Paintbrushes
It's good to have a few different-sized paintbrushes. Always clean your paintbrush when you've finished.

Glue
We use PVA glue in most of these projects, because it is strong and easy to apply.

Scissors
Use child-size scissors. Ask an adult to help you with any tricky bits.

Ribbon, string or cotton
To hang up your decorations. Any colour will do.

Paper Pet Chains

You will need:

Paper approx. 60 cm x 10 cm
Ruler
Pencil
Scissors
Colouring pens
Scrap pieces of coloured paper,
    glitter and glue to decorate

Decorate your room with these cute paper pals. You can use your own pet as inspiration, or dream up a new creature to hang on your walls.

1

Fold the piece of paper backwards and forwards into a concertina shape, making sure that the folds are 10 cm wide.

2

Draw the picture of your pet on the top fold. The picture must touch both sides of the paper. This will make sure that all the pets are linked together.

Paper chains aren't just great for your bedroom, they are also a fantastic way to decorate a room for parties. Just draw a picture that matches the theme and cut out to create the perfect party paper chains.

4

Decorate each pet shape using your colouring pens, glitter or cut out pieces of paper. You can make each one the same, or all different.

3

Cut out the shape using scissors and open out.

Animal Masks

Go wild with this lion mask! But don't stop there - why not make a happy hippo or an exotic bird of paradise?

You will need:
Orange and yellow paper plates
Scissors
Blu tack or plasticine
A sharp pencil
Glue
Tissue paper
Colouring pens
Hole punch
String or elastic

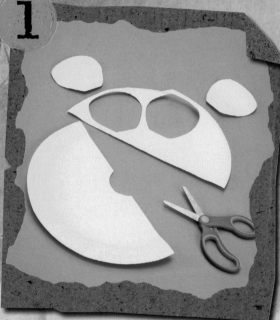

Cut the yellow plate in half. In one half, cut out a small 'n' shape in the middle of the flat side to fit around your nose. Use the other half to cut out two ears and a nose.

2

Put blu tack under the plate where you want eyeholes. Carefully push a sharp pencil through the paper plate into the blu tack. Ask an adult to cut an eye shape. Repeat to make the other eye.

3

Cut the orange plate into 8 segments. Glue these orange pieces around the yellow plate to make the mane. Then glue the yellow ears and nose on.

4

Cut slits into a length of tissue paper to make some extra mane. Glue this behind the paper mane. Draw around the edges with colouring pens to make the features stand out.

5

Use your hole punch to make holes at the side of the mask. Tie string or elastic on and it's ready to wear!

Concertina Butterflies

You will need:
Coloured card
Scissors
6 sheets of A4-sized tissue paper
Stapler
Sticky tape
Hole punch
Coloured ribbon or string

Make fluttering butterflies, soaring birds, and other fun flying creatures to hang from your ceiling. We will be making a beautiful butterfly, but you can use the same technique to make any winged creature you can think of!

1

Draw the shape of a butterfly's body onto the coloured card and cut out.

2

Lay three pieces of tissue paper on top of each other and fold them backwards and forwards as if you were making a fan. Repeat with the other three pieces of tissue.

3

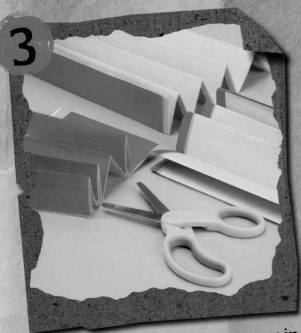

Cut the folded bits of tissue paper in 2 to make 4 pieces. Make sure that 2 pieces are longer than the other 2.

4

Fan out each tissue paper piece and staple in place on the card butterfly body.

5

Cut out another piece of card, slightly smaller than the butterfly body, and glue on top of the pink body. Make a hole in the top of the head using the hole punch. Tie some ribbon through the hole and hang your butterfly up.

11

Robot Weaving

Make a robot with a colourful circuit board tummy by weaving with coloured pieces of paper. You can make your robots different shapes and sizes – just use your imagination to create a fantastic team of robots.

You will need:
A4 grey card
Black colouring pen
Scissors
Ruler
Coloured paper cut into
1 cm wide strips

1

Fold the card in half, lengthways, and draw half a robot. Draw one leg, one arm, half a body and half a head as shown above.

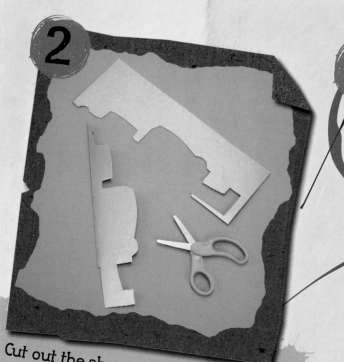

Cut out the shape of the robot and keep it folded in half.

Using your ruler, draw lines on the body of your robot that are about 1 cm apart. Cut along the lines.

Open out the robot. Weave the coloured lengths of paper in and out of the slits you have cut. Switch from starting under to over for each slit.

Cut the ends of the coloured paper strips so they don't show. Draw on the details of your robot with the black colouring pen.

Mosaic Minibeasts

You don't need to travel to ancient Rome to enjoy mosaics. Make your own using any paper you can find and cutting it into small squares. Recycle scraps of wrapping paper, old birthday cards or magazines to create your minibeast masterpiece.

1 Cut the pieces of scrap paper into 2 cm wide strips and then cut each strip into small squares that are roughly the same size.

2 Stick the squares of coloured paper onto the white A4 paper leaving a small gap between each square.

You can use your mosaic minibeasts to decorate almost anything. Stick them on notebooks, cards or mount them in a frame.

4

Cut the shapes out. Repeat all the steps to make more mosaics for your minibeasts scene. You will need some leaves, a caterpillar, butterfly and dragonfly. Stick all of these onto the black piece of card.

3

Make a stencil by drawing a flower shape on a piece of paper. Cut it out and draw around it two times on the mosaic.

15

Stapled Paper Hearts

These lovely decorations are perfect to make and hang in your window. You could use sparkly paper to make them really catch the light.

Try using smaller pieces of paper to make mini versions. They are perfect to use as fancy gift tags.

You will need:
Coloured paper
Scissors
Stapler
Cotton or string
Sticky tape

1

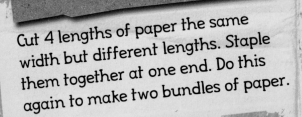

Cut 4 lengths of paper the same width but different lengths. Staple them together at one end. Do this again to make two bundles of paper.

2

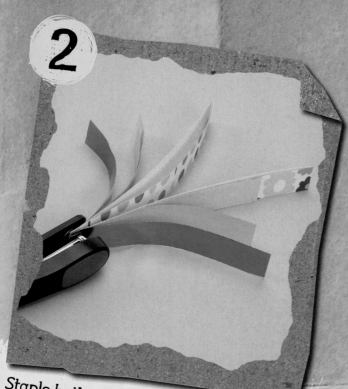

Staple both of the paper bundles together making sure the shortest lengths are on the outside.

3

Fold the strips of paper on one side half down towards the stapled end of the bundles. Line the edges up and staple the strips to the bundle.

4

Repeat on the other side to make the heart shape and staple to fix in place.

5

Make three hearts in total. Attach a short piece of cotton to the top of each heart with sticky tape. Stick them altogether to make a string of hearts, ready to hang.

Shoebox Swamp

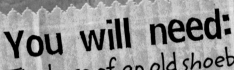

You will need:
The base of an old shoebox
Paint
Paintbrush
Coloured paper or card
Scissors
Black colouring pen
Glue

Transform an old shoebox into a super swamp filled with overhanging trees, lily pads and a hopping frog.

1

Paint your shoe box. Paint green on the bottom and blue on the top, sides and outside.

2

Using different shades of green paper, cut out a wavy shape for some hills and a spiky shape for the grass.

3

Using other coloured paper, cut out a pond, lily pads, clouds, trees, reeds and flowers.

Try creating different scenes, such as a planet-filled outer space theme with zooming rockets.

4

Glue the pond, hills and clouds in first. Then stick the trees on the side.

5

Cut out a shape of a frog from some green card. Draw the frog's features using a black colouring pen. Add the frog to your scene along with any other small details such as flowers and reeds. Your scene is complete!

Fruity Fridge Magnets

Foil is a great material to mould into any shape. Make any fridge magnets you like. Why not try some letters or numbers?

Decorate the outside of your fridge with these fun food magnets! Use them to attach handy notes to the fridge or to display pieces of art you have just made.

You will need:
Tin foil
Tissue paper
PVA glue
Paintbrush
Black colouring pen
Magnets
Double-sided sticky tape

1

Scrunch up a piece of tin foil (about 50 cm long) and shape it into a strawberry (which is similar to a heart shape).

2

Cover the whole shape in small pieces of red tissue paper using PVA glue. Leave to dry in a warm space.

3

Draw some pips onto the strawberry using the black colouring pen.

4

Cut out 5 leaf shapes with long stems out of green tissue paper. Twist them altogether and glue them on top of the strawberry.

5

Using double-sided tape or glue, stick a magnet to the back of the strawberry. When it is dry you can use it to stick to a fridge or any metal surface.

Tissue Paper Sunlight Catchers

You will need:
Plastic pocket
Tissue paper
PVA glue
Black colouring pen
Scissors
Hole punch
Cotton thread

Make your very own stained glass sunlight catchers that will twinkle and sparkle in the light.

2

Glue them onto a plastic pocket in a random pattern using the PVA glue. Leave to dry in a warm place until completely dry. This could take up to 24 hours.

1

Cut lots of different shapes out of tissue paper, or rip some into small squares.

3

Make a template of a star. Draw around this template onto your tissue paper pattern using a black colouring pen.

4

Cut out all your shapes. You can cut out just stars, or you could cut out different shapes, too.

5

Stick a length of cotton on top of the stars using sticky tape and hang up!

Glossary

concertina a shape made by folding paper backwards and forwards

magnet a metal material that sticks to other metal materials

mane the long hair around a lion's neck

masterpiece a fantastic piece of artwork

minibeast a small animal such as an a bee, ladybird, beetle or spider

mosaic a picture made from lots of smaller bits of paper, tiling or glass

paper chains decorations made by joining pieces of paper together

template a shape you can draw around again and again to make the same shape

tissue paper very thin paper often used as wrapping paper

swamp a very muddy pond or lake

Index

Other titles in this series:

WAYLAND